BOW

Penelope Austin

BOW

Published by Slope Editions
www.slopeeditions.org

Grateful acknowledgment is made to the editors of the following
magazines in which these poems originally appeared:

"Dancing After Oswiecim": *Kenyon Review*
"The State I Loved You In": *Ploughshares*
"Romance of the Road": *The Journal*
"Heedless": *The New Republic*
"Unless You Think": *Tampa Review*
"On Woodward Avenue, Detroit" and "Another Autumn": *Quarterly West*
"Snowstorm Above Lord's Valley: Case Study in the Psychobiology of
Failure" and "Interstice": *Orion*
"Moon Under the Twenties," "Clandestine," "Azaleas," and "Aubade:
No Time for Nice Touches": *The Missouri Review*

LIBRARY OF CONGRESS CATALOGING-IN-PUBLICATION DATA
Austin, Penelope.
Bow / Penelope Austin.
p. cm.
ISBN-10   0-9777698-2-8
ISBN-13   978-0-9777698-2-7
1. Cancer in women—Poetry. I. Title.
PS3551.U87B69 2008
811'.54—dc22   2008005318

Book design by Amy Borezo
www.shelterbookworks.com
Text set in LTC Cloister Pro

10 9 8 7 6 5 4 3 2 1

[B]ut suppose your nature was quixotic, impulsive, altruistic, guileless; suppose you were a hungry man starving for something to love and lean upon, for one whose burdens you might bear, and who might help you to bear yours. Suppose you were down on your luck, still stunned by a horrible shock, and this bright vista of a happy future floated suddenly before you, how long under these circumstances do you think you would reflect before you would decide on embracing what change had thrown in your way?

Samuel Butler, *The Way of All Flesh*

CONTENTS

xi   *Introduction*

Snowstorm

3   Snowstorm Above Lord's Valley:
       Case Study in the Psychobiology of Failure

6   Snow Removal, 3 A.M.

7   Life Is But a—

8   Field

9   Matter

11   She Turns

13   Jaskinia Rai

15   On Woodward Avenue, Detroit

17   Under My Tongue

19   Moon Above the Twenties

21   Dancing After Oswiecim

22   Laws of Sound and Light

23   The Politics of Loving a Nice Guy

26   Aubade: No Time for Nice Touches

27   Big Beauty

The Reach

33 Clandestine
34 Implicate Order I
37 The State I Loved You In
39 My Daughter Rejects Walt Whitman in
    Her Mother's Library
42 Romance of the Road
44 Living Proof: Sonnets
52 My Daughter Reads Me a Political
    Poem of the Nineties
54 Revision
56 Her Song, Chemotherapy
58 I Remodel Nancy Carducci's House
61 Interstice
63 Azaleas
65 Implicate Order II

What I Bear

69 Heedless
70 Another Autumn
71 Nuts
74 Band Rock
76 Last Blue Moon of the Millennium
78 Lenticchie in Umido
82 Actuarial Tables
86 Farewell to the Flesh
90 Beauty/Truth
92 Plum/Age
94 Unless You Think

Introduction

In May of 2003 Penelope Austin and her husband Chris Bastress stopped at our house in Vermont, on their way home after seeing Penny's daughter Alexandra graduate from the Berklee School of Music. Penny was not in good shape, that was clear. She had been battling cancer for almost 20 years, and was determined to see Alexandra graduate. Just before she and Chris left, she gave me the manuscript of *Bow*. She asked that if I thought anyone might be interested in publishing it, I should feel free to send it their way. She died in Ann Arbor a month later.

I had known Penny for the many years she had been fighting to keep her cancer at bay. She was one of the most active people I ever met. She raised her daughter, taught aerobics, led poetry workshops for both healthy and terminally ill cancer patients, worked on and received her PhD from the University of Utah, and still found time to dance circles around the rest of us when the music was from Motown, her hometown.

Penny was an extraordinary cook, willing to put together a four-course meal at the drop of a hat, or a hint that some nice wine might be in the offing. As she says in her poem "Lenticchie in Umido," "I must be everything I want myself." Her cooking reflected not only her love of life, but her quest for perfection in all things. Not to mention her extraordinary hospitality. I mention this in part because cooking shows up in many of these poems.

Penny was educated at the University of Michigan, the University of Missouri, the University of Utah, and St. Hilda's College of Oxford University. Her first book, *Waiting for a Hero*, was published in 1988 by the University of Missouri Press. It was a spectacular debut, playing off her namesake, Penelope, who waits for her husband-hero, Odysseus. During her lifetime, her poems appeared in *American Poetry Review*, *The New Republic*, *Ploughshares*, *The Kenyon Review*, *Orion*, and many others.

These poems are a testament to her will to live. Some of them deal directly with her cancer, and many of them do not. The fact that she wrote them at all while in so much pain is surely a miracle. The poems here both ask and answer questions, sometimes in the same poem. They play off each other in a way almost never seen in a book of poems, which is part of what makes *Bow* a real book rather than a posthumous collection.

Another thing that sets *Bow* apart from many poetry collections is its reach. The second section of the book is titled "The Reach," and its epigraph is from Roger Shattuck's *Forbidden Knowledge: From Prometheus to Pornography*, which reads, in part, "At their purest, ideas are disembodied and timeless. We need ideas to reason logically and to explore the fog of uncertainty that surrounds the immediate encounter with daily living." I can't think of another book that tackles this issue of embodying the pure idea—of *performing* one's thoughts—so surely and movingly.

These are not small, incidental poems. They are big poems that take chances, poems that expect the reader to shudder at some of their conclusions, to think again about what poetry can do.

Though she was warm and friendly to a fault, Penny could also be intellectually daunting. To a degree, her poems follow suit.

"Living Proof" is a crown of sonnets titled by year, beginning in 1996 and ending with 1958, skipping among 60's sit-ins, the wars of countries and sexes, the changes in the narrator's life and in the world around her. The first poem begins with "I haven't the capacity for war," and the twelfth one ends with the same line (thus a crown). Not a big fan of confessional poetry, Penny manages in this brilliant sequence to so impress the reader with her formal agility that we are unaware at first that we are learning a great deal about her.

Some of the poems here address Penny's physical decline, as in "My Daughter Reads Me a Political Poem of the Nineties":

> My feet grow to look
> like Oriental succulents, like gingerroot,
> my nose a big bottomed pear, not Ruby Bosc, but Bartlett.
> I consider the recipe for pears in ginger sauce, and lick
> my finger to turn the page just as my mother might.

Or this, from "Her Song, Chemotherapy," a poem about a maid singing while cleaning rooms:

> I listened to her song in the cold-surfaced Hilton,
> I listened to her song ignorant of my illness.
> It took me much farther along than that morning
>
> I had thought I was ready to go.

Penelope Austin lived a full and complex life and wrote poems to match it. This book is a record of both facing death and facing life, both of which she did with a grace not often found in this world. I cannot express how happy I am that Slope Editions had the good judgment to publish it. I want to thank everyone there for their help in seeing *Bow* into the world. I know that Penny would be thrilled, especially by the tire tracks on the cover.

Wyn Cooper

SNOWSTORM

Anyone who has faced death will know precisely what I am referring to, perhaps because the irreversibility of death focuses our thoughts sharply on the monumental scale of the human minded life. It should not take death, however, to make anyone sensitive to this issue. Life should be enough to make us approach the human mind with respect for its dignity and stature, and, almost paradoxically, with tenderness for its fragility.

The feeling of what happens is the answer to a question we never asked, and it is also the coin in a Faustian bargain that we could never have negotiated. Nature did it for us.

> Antonio R. Damasio, *The Feeling of What Happens: Body and Emotion in the Making of Consciousness*

SNOWSTORM ABOVE LORD'S VALLEY: CASE STUDY IN THE PSYCHOBIOLOGY OF FAILURE

Where I call for you, infinite, and dispersed,
                    I am heading into flat light, thin as mica.
Up here, winter minutes splice sense data of primary imagination. Even as

my cold windshield receives snowflakes, fingerprints of invisible hosts—
                    who chant on high in this wind—
bulging snow clouds bear down

                    round as tender heels in the grip of loss, digging in
          for redemption.
                    I bear down with gritted teeth. Salt, silt, sand—

such grit abrades the trying pavement—and who is so very certain
                    the wounds that send me reeling are so much the
     better for the pain?

Cold as Mother Nature atop this mountain
above Lord's Valley or Promised Land. Taillights ahead—
                    small comforts—vanish,

          the last something
                    to grasp, an image, and finally a *seeing redly*
around the curve ahead,

abandoning me to swirl and blizzard, invisible road
     again—Isn't this enough mystery?—The black car skids downhill,
          stirs up snow ghosts before the windshield, ghosts rising and falling,

ghosts mooning over ice as barren as a short life.
Frightened, I choose to believe when I think
ghosts, I have a soul.

Sadly, I choose to believe that to think is to have.
How could I lose you in answers?
The spiraling bodily curve of consciousness fills me with awe, lifts

my head to the sky. Careering blind,
as is my way, I sing
Be Thou my vision.

My sky gives way to dark equinoxes
of thought, of cloud, of harmony. The feeling of what happens—
hands on the leather steering wheel, the slow descent, warily, on the highway,

semi-articulated eighteen-wheelers right-passing, intrepid in the gloom and
slush.
Naught be all else to me save
I let myself slide here

to bring sorrow to an end. Headlights throw a curve
of light ahead as far as the fragile trellis of snow
hooding my car. In this globe

of reflected light, I am no less
for love, I am not seeing earth begin again.
Then out of Lord's Valley. On the radio

a cello hollows an arc in some New Age affirmation concerto
and I'm ready to believe

that Scranton is all I desired after all (the slick road, the hairpin curve,
the direct descent),

                         that desire's tired of being in poems.
The body files *way* and *will* when memory won't, pulls them
up out of the dark,

where I call for you,

                        infinite, and dispersed, red lights
fishtailing on the curves.

SNOW REMOVAL, 3 A.M.

Falling back into out of

the body space I catch
a jagged drone, moan
of a ghost machine, churning

the near distance. Obscure,
industrious, impolite
as an earthworm, it works

somewhere below sleep.
A plume of snow, I can believe,
bows

against the sky's black page.
La plume. By day penned in

graceless matter
of our lumpy bodies
the heart rises. Where
does the white go

in spring? Such machinations
we go through to turn
our souls from black to white.
Isn't that why we take

our pens in hand?
The heart arcs
toward beauty, trailing
stars in its wake.

Edging toward the hole cut
in the opaque ice, she could hardly
make out the words
of the fishermen: gutturals
and long-drawled vowels,
language of hills and hollows, of hiding,
not of open books. Or dust. The men
ringed the fire
burning on the ice
as the glow licked
the rim of a cut
incised above the lake's black water.
Where fire and ice touched, the edge
softened into lack of distinction. The men
huddled in their tattered orange parkas and turned
their gray gloves over and over
above the flames, hawking and spitting
into shadows beyond
the ring
of fire.
Black lines strewn across the ice hung empty.
Her wool scarf chafed against dry
skin of her cheeks. She ran her tongue
around her chapped lips once more
as she joined the circle of men
keeping warm by the fire.

FIELD

Our road girdles bottomland
between blue hills rising from a bruise
of clouds—just like paradise or islands—

and the placid and polluted
Susquehanna etched
in its course. Swollen, the river spills

over banks, stirs submerged detritus
anchored in its current.
In November, the field sinks, shorn

of its cornstalks and Queen Anne's lace.
Mature, flattened, the plain lies
fallow, offering merely stubble

and stones, nothing profound or grand,
gray as the sky, its prosaic history.
The cold land spreads out here,

a common specimen stunned senseless,
pinned between beauty and violence,
but not dead yet. The ground trembles,

going nowhere as a great train rumbles
in its predictable tracks across
vast undifferentiated landscapes

toward the vanishing point.

MATTER

She holds the key
clicking like crickets against
her teeth. Long skirts skirl dust-
motes floating thin as script. Air
veins down on the desert's gold
lodes humped under rock.
Heels tap folly, folly, folly

while pock-skinned lizards skim quick
as thought at her approach. She encroaches
on the vast red past, unlocks:
Screens, rickety frames, dust pans,
crushed plastic water bottles, bicycle gears,
sieves and sifters cantilevered
in the dry-webbed dark. Picks and three-pronged rakes
clack and skitter in the dim gleam.

At her elbow debris hovers
apologetically as clerks figuring
their books. She kneels
to her inspection and scratches
in the dust. Fingers grow
into the floorboards. Splinters' racket
cracks heat. Light blooms.
Its shape spills onto rock.
Butte, mesa turn brass.
Brass turns poppy, poppy bone,

white as teeth. Mouth blooms poppy.
Smoke crisscrosses her view, catches strands

of her hair. She wraps the key
in a corner of the landscape.
It anchors the dust. Trumpet-flowers sift down
onto her shoulders. The desert moves her
imperceptibly. It breathes liquid brass air.

SHE TURNS

into the wonder of it, the wonder   disseminating, the wonder a slow heat,
heat of embarrassment, of guilt,   a wide yawn or
       wind over grass
and down the drive—or up?
The house at the end—is the door open?
Yes, wide, a lawn,
                the opening. If it is something
                like death, it turns her
out of its pocket,
    wind rushing   through the hole,
      lint skittering down her thigh, her shin,
        collecting in her shoe, her boot,
her blue pill cracked in half   and swallowed like pain itself eased
                 into the blue, the blue
of rails glanced in sun, rails stretched on on on,   the distance opened
              like a yawn—
the vanishing point—   a pinprick like
angels
    (: balanced poised on its steel head—   breathtaking!)
      now leaking through   the hole into the light
like fireflies themselves—"exactly   like the bubbles in
Champagne"—
    and so it must be spring at least or summer,   this ache, this opening,
the use of it all, the warm air pushed   out of the winter balloon, the wonder.
Miscellany: A cracked smile.
Pulse. Pulses and legumes clattering together   into the All-Clad.
More water. A good soaking.
Night and tittering. To-whit to-whoo.   Oh, *The Island* of the here & now.
Romance sometimes the cold heat   the most she feels, the slight trail
Of butterfly wing, slug's cellophane, oh,   and that little gesture
    of brushing away, brushing away,   as if at delusion, not memory.

Torn between admiration for cold pots' quick flare at the touch of flame
(the blue metal)   and the content of cobwebs,
or mold, settling on milkweed pods
or in the crotches of trees (such as: redbuds), between hard fear and passive
                    acceptance—
which is love?—she turns
a page, runs   her finger across the words, parallel to truth,
between words,   blank rivers
splitting the pages,   those rivers
exactly the rivers   she will never travel (because they don't exist),
those rivers, she has faith,   she will travel, those rivers
                              the rivers of angels
pulsing there, just there,   fallen through the hole, just there,
                    behind the abstract house, the open door
the wonder rising up   behind it.   She turns.

JASKINIA RAI

Lie still in my low bark.
Easter lilies line my throat.

Ancient stones are not ruins,
And the militant men of my heart

Have left for the sea. Wave on wave
I lisp night sounds. Sibilance

Takes the last light of day.
Lie on. Lie on. This is

The last light. The country
Is foreign and breathes

An unknown language. I can learn.
Dogs and pickaxes crowd in.

The mosaic on the floor has grown
Too colorful, the honeysuckle

Unmanageable, wings of hair
Wisp across seabluffs.

Later I rake hay on a Polish farm.
A low hum is random.

I want capture but deny kings
Their claims on the land.

We don't know castles yet.
We've never seen candles. The new

Race grows from the bottom
Of the cave. How the rounded

Lengths of stone push into the dark
Steady drip along the green

And pink walls before the lights
Go out, and we stumble toward pools

To drink from crude bowls left behind.
Fire has been discovered by now.

The light outside is stunning.

Jaskinia Rai is a cave in southern Poland where bones of a
Neanderthal village were found in the 1960s.

ON WOODWARD AVENUE, DETROIT

> *It was just my imagination*
> *Runnin' away with me.*
>> The Temptations

There's talk of angels
among us, wing and prayer in a mirror
(imagine, that tells without reflecting),
as when nothing lies between us
and stars come up. The sun fades

I don't mean to frighten you.
I don't mean to frighten you

because there's talk of angels.
among us, stars come up. The sun fades.
See, yourself, in the mirror:
Nothing lies between us,

unless your wing deflecting
my prayer. I pray without reflecting.

I don't mean to frighten you.
Nothing lies between us
if there's talk of angels'
telling glimpse of wing in mirror

and stars come up. The sun fades.
The sun fades. Stars come up.

Night bleeds to benign light reflecting
wings' scars like scraps of prayers in the mirror.

I don't mean to frighten you.
  There's talk of angels

    when nothing lies between us.
    When nothing lies between us

  the sun fades. Stars come up,
though there's talk of angels.
Wing to prayer, prayer to wing, we reflect.
  I don't mean to frighten you.

    Winter wings hold up the mirror—
    tell me what breath forms on the mirror—

    Nothing lies between us.
  I don't mean to frighten you.
The sun fades. Stars come up.
At the point of least reflection
  there's breath of angels.

Stars fade. The sun comes up.
  There's talk of nothing between us.
I don't mean to frighten you. Angels lie.

for Wyn

UNDER MY TONGUE

I am Moscow today.
        My eyes brim full of St. Basil's
    long-winded centuries flaring
banners outside my lecture halls,
            stewing in my furnace rooms,
    the conflagration of staring
postlapsarian walls,

lackadaisical, unsealed tombs.
            Streets, lines, hairs, the cold:
    Call it growing old,
if you will. The city stalks on,
            flinging its astrakhan
    aside as it comes into the future.
Today I am the future.

        (This submerged city.
    This submerged country.)
I travel like the daughter of a deposed
            head of state, carrying my mother's jewels
    under my tongue.

Oceans of citizens move across
            my face. I am at a loss
    in this contemporary milieu.
How easy it is to misconstrue
            the designs of nature, the lesions
    of temporary actuality, the legions
of miscalculations, misplaced

and generally untraced
                    affection, limitations
          of imitations. Or intimations.
Slips of the tongue. The mother
                    tongue, to be precise. I am
          Moscow today. Inside I am
kneeling for hours. The chanters

sing in a minor key. Stained
                    glass light filters in. Inside the saints
          are jeweled. They rise, they rise.
Jewels scatter across the vestibule,
                    a myriad of gold charms and jewels,
          scattering, scattering, somewhere
at the center.

MOON ABOVE THE TWENTIES

Cool argument, but no less cool the evening,
the night's illogical statement its blatant moon
pasted full against the sky and rising,

pale, tooled face blind as justice. Still
it holds our attention beyond any tired
appearances elsewhere, so night after blessed night

we round our lips and point, Oh, look, look,
the moon. Here it is, the argument: Following
the fiery collision or convulsion (though

there are those who still insist it was
a voice that caused the conflagration), the flames
died down, the surface cooled and corrugated.

Mountains pushed up from the land. Grass, trees,
and the crocus pushed up from the soil, each stem
vying for greater height or succumbing to a lesser

place. Oceans receded, ships were set to sail.
All this is evidence for this century
when the invisible showed itself as real,

subatomic particles the proof
that what we cannot see can be our fall.
So factories pushed up from farms and villages.

Hundreds of men left their pedestrian dreams
and bent to one. How were we in short
hair and silk stockings able to choose

one among them? One man, one task, assembling
pistons that powered the supreme American privacy
down the road—with luck, perhaps, veering

off the beaten path and up above
a city's lights pixilating in
the rarified atmosphere where we turn to the one

beside us, love blurred to mercy in that light:
"Oh, look, look, the moon. It's full. It's ours."
And we believe it is above all else.

We're shown the dust of our graves behind glass.
      Then the pictures of our murderers.
           Death is our common possession, they say,
forgetting that nakedness common
      to the dispossessed. Here death is the property
           of angels; nakedness the property of men.
So we are forced to huddle naked together
      in the small chamber, trampling children beneath us,
           and until we take leave of our senses completely,
our last sense is touch: another naked body
      against ours. So we leave as we have come in,
           unaccommodated, our thousand pairs of shoes,
our suitcases, and our hair on display,
      leave our nakedness as our legacy, the source
           of all our need and our desire on this earth.

A few hours later in Zakopane, we drink in
      the healthful mountain air, and we drink
           the health of the couple dressed to the teeth
who are celebrating their second anniversary.
      In a highland hut, to Tartary tunes, we dance.
           My father rises from his wheelchair to sway
with Grace, his nurse, and the bus driver clicks
      his tongue softly as he lifts me in the steps
           of the polka. I wear a silver skirt that wraps
around us, sandals, and tie back my hair
      in a pink band. We dance with abandon,
           and the bus driver loves me, and we all press
in the light and the heat of the fire. Ah, Zakopane.
      To your cross on Gasprowy Mountain! To your feather
           beds, our common nakedness, the soft clicking all night!

> *It is because this process is fluid that phenomenalism comes to grief. It is not that physical objects lurk behind a veil which we can never penetrate. It is rather that every apparent situation which we take as verifying or falsifying the statements which we make about them leaves other possibilities open.*

A.J. Ayer, *The Problem of Knowledge*

Fold your clothes over the chair,
　　your shirt by my skirt,
　　　　your jeans, my silk blouse.
　　The way sound and light travel,

I know only what you leave behind:
　　a reasonable facsimile.
　　　　So turn out the light
　　and quick!—

before our eyes adjust.
　　Darkness blinds laws of reason,
　　　　and unless your touch can mute moonlight,
　　madness is out of the question.

THE POLITICS OF LOVING A NICE GUY

*Certainly there are some things which I can find out about you
only, or best, through being told of them by you.*

Gilbert Ryle, *Concept of Mind*

I

Amid the tinkle and clink of ice cubes in drinks
slid across the red stippled confetti-strewn bar
in Franco's, amid the friends and year-end fracas,

eggplant balloons strung languidly loose from booths,
barstools askew across the aisle, Ariana tilting a tray
of booze breast-high, cresting the breaking crowd, loud

in revelry, the ex-wife surfaces, stunningly resplendent
in designer dancewear, aerobically fit at forty, deigning
to tip a smile toward my tight lips flecked with beer foam.

Ah, the Dear One, he greets her sweetly, sweeping his hand
toward my table, taking pains to introduce us all, his gaze
resting a millisecond too long on my long gone to seed

plumpness, my smeary mascara, stemming ejaculatory gossip. Oh,
the Nice Guy, he places a chaste kiss on the ex-wife's lips
and heels into a delicate cheek-to-cheek holiday hug.

My over-the-hill Jills mug at me, and I shrug against my impulse
to cry, I who admire my nice guy and do advocate civility. Shit,
I'm only human. How'd he come to succumb to cool-headed
niceties?

Surely some surreptitious shred of automatic sexual response
must rear its head from its coiled past, its underlying bed
of stimulus-reaction, appearing shadowy and real as the skeleton

beneath the body's fleshly outlines in an x-ray. X-wife, x-love,
explain the ebb of even anger once anchored rancorous and red
like a boot battened to a misparked car to keep it in its place.

Some degree of passionlessness in the polite and politic rankles.
I sniff and preen my mood with pride, let him know I'm miffed.
And he's right to take umbrage, has got the gumption to upbraid

my infelicitous behavior. Queen Bee and the Blue Hornet Band
honey in the blues. It'll be awhile before the Nice Guy and I
lock bones and tongues, lay loin to loin, see jointly eye-to-eye.

II
Last September, a next-door neighbor lit a fire near our fence,
dousing already two-foot flames with fresh draughts of gasoline.
Lashing out, fire singed her brows, burned her eyes. She flung

the gas can away into the drought-dry grass, which gave itself
to little licking tendrils of fire snaking across her lawn.
We caught her voice singing up to us as we lay sighing in sleep

a window away. Taking the stairs down two at a time, berobed
and barefoot, he woke fully to panic, leaping the picket fence,
our garden hose in tow, to frustrate the fire, stunt its growth,

while other neighbors lined the walk to watch. Once confident
of safety, he sought out the neighbor still screaming inside
her house and offered her a ride to the ER. In my nightie,

I waited while he dressed, I saw the doors shut, heard the locks
turned against him in the house he saved. Every subsequent
Saturday, the neighbors set their burn barrel ablaze, oblivious

to their luck in living by a nice guy, blind to the blackened
rings of bare ground bearing witness to their near miss, the kiss
of disaster arising from gas added to already inflamed matter.

III

Lately, I've been contemplating the distance between language
and passion: our blows and kisses bleed into abstractions;
the Old Country's onion domes flavor our Christmas Eve feasts,

civility makes our goodness a matter of manners. Well-versed
in lip-service to misspent youth, irresistible yous, and the use
of effective contraceptives, I came slowly to the revelation that

a guy who was nice to others would be likely to be nice to me.
*The boxer, the surgeon, the poet and the salesman apply their
special criteria in the performance of their special tasks, for*

they are trying to get things right. So it is with nice guys.
It's simply not easy to live with. Niceness points up nastiness
in the less than nice (me), notices goodness thrives on moisture,

not heat, on plenty, but never on too much. *Overt intelligent
performances are not clues to the workings of minds; they are
those workings.* He comes home to me, oh me, in my prickliness.

I can rejoice in his generosity, evidence of my judicious choice;
yet I keep in mind he's had thirty flat tires: slow leaks, burned
rubber, or blowouts born of driving his car too hard over risk.

AUBADE: NO TIME FOR NICE TOUCHES

Small wonder I've maligned you, old fool,
     and your untimeliness. Either too early
        or too late you condescend to this
beleaguered earth as if its own revolutions

have nothing to do with temperance.
     So too hot too soon one pink and tender
        tulip pushes up through the cold bed
of the garden against all earthly desire

to lie, still, dormant, subterranean.
     This is no time for nice touches. Too fast
        the flower moves into the season and won't last
against the old wind blowing in from the West

or the blight of an April freeze
     beneath the skull of the land—though that type,
        I'm told, blooms early and dies young. But I
can forgive you when I see the hardy forsythia

braving it out by the roadside. Perhaps not
     all is nipped by the climate. Along that road
        seasons race south, making time a matter
of geography. And by the time we travel

that road, the whole land will swelter
     under the spell of heat, the compass rose
        full-blown, the fields ripe. So temper me.
This year I can weather the early spring.

BIG BEAUTY

You cannot miss her big beauty as she
leans forward from the silver gelatin print.
My daughter is the lightest thing, pinpointed

like the sunbleached city radiating
at the vee of sloping goldenrod-
and paintbrush-dotted mountains of the canyon.

Bare arms folded across her jeans she sits
amid the ragamuffin kids of West
Branch School for peace and love. I don't say this

because I am her mother. This is what
the photograph tells me. Today my doctor
tells me: "You will die from this." She says

my daughter should be with me when I pass
away. I have been imagining
that day, its bigness in my daughter's life.

I will say: "Oh, love, what you have been
to me. Mountains, sun, and flowers. I've loved
you as the silver road, as the glimpse

of farmland from a plane, as cobalt cliffs
emerging from the bluish mist beyond
the coast of Borneo. I have loved you

as noon light on the stucco walls of lost
and renamed cities, as the brazen flash
of bougainvilleas, the copper in your hair,

as the prayer of bullfrogs sung at midnight
in Singapore, as rusty fantasies
of rock against a purple Utah sky,

as bracing water tumbling over moss
at World's End, as sun disappearing
behind the Endless Mountains, and as all

these children gathered in the picture, smiling
into their futures. I have loved you as you
appear in this memento: radiant,

centered." How can I not take that with me?

THE REACH

How can we be faithful and unfaithful at the same time?

At their purest, ideas are disembodied and timeless. We need ideas to reason logically and to explore the fog of uncertainty that surrounds the immediate encounter with daily living. Equally we need stories to embody the medium of time in which human character takes shape and reveals itself to us, and in which we discover our own mortality.

Roger Shattuck, *Forbidden Knowledge: From Prometheus to Pornography*

We are entering the season of the interior.
           Oh, heavens, the groundcover tangles greenly
               among the lilies of the valley and the hills
     bear up their frieze of frenzied leaves

just at the limit of sight. The downward
          spiral of desire begins here. I am not
             afraid of growing old, but rather of returning
    to the season of youth each year a little

more worn, a little more tried by winter.
           Where does this begin? With the taking off
            of coats, of sweaters, with baring legs?
   With flesh and all its whiteness, the plump

and timid shoulder behind the first sleeveless
         summer dress, toes and knees stained with grass?
             Then the earth's body turns itself inside out,
    distending its colorful organs, hot pinks

and the pulsing hearts of peonies crawling
        with ants. At night I go long-limbed
           for the voices breathing up from earth:
   Flesh is nothing. The scar of mountains,

the cracked beds of dried up rivers nothing.
       I am not young, but I try on the word *twig*.
        I am not innocent, but I try on the word *tendril,*
   the word *summer.*

The subject of all poetry
is death, the adorable young poet says,
trim and lithe, dark, intense,
repeating the reputable critic. *I mean*
what else is there? Name me

a subject. The audience gets shifty.
When death enters, all is luminous.
Lorca. I happen to know. All
is the moment intensified—as rain
on shale at the curve of a mountain,

as sun on one glistening point
of the mass catches, the mass itself
the one glistening point of the edifice
built on stone, the outpouring litany,
the expiration, the attention, the candle

one glistening point of the human heart,
snuffing oxygen as it burns, the tension
of the flame. The point is too small.
How fine, *fine*, finally the moment
of absolute separation and how

dangerous. Once we separate point
from point from point we are bound
to compare: Which point more

luminous? Which perception more true?
The moment of death is not luminous.

The ultimate blur, concrete in abstract,
death is the moment of peace that comes
without compare. If the poem is
the luminous moment of the awareness
of the reality of death, then it is

too small a thing, poised. *This* is
the subject of all poetry: our lack
of perspective, the squint that renders buds
of the shag bark hickory indistinguishable
from crabapple buds, the pink and tender

flowers of the cherry, streaking, flattened,
against the mountain falling away
in rain, glistening, yes, but on it all.
This too blurs with my hands on the steering
wheel, nothing indistinct in my vision,

and so with my hands on the keys here,
black letters thus the words not distinct
from the screen, each word implied
by space and time and *sense*, distinction
shaking out as the pastime of the idle,

the dying, the eye that does not see
the threads behind the fabric, tying
all into one flat landscape,

luminous in time and space, undoable,
unravellable, all equal. The subject

of all poetry is death for all
poetry contains death and it
contains and is contained by
all that is that is not death,
adorable, trim, dark, repeating.

THE STATE I LOVED YOU IN

A low sound in the hollows
fills low places, fills hollows,
carves a hollow from the right place
or hollows being in place,
a sound I heard
in a strange place,
in a strange state,
just off the road in southern Utah,
just over the border, just off the desert,
where a field of wheat ran gold
into the sun as if it were a bright day in February,
where a half ring of black boulders rose by the road
where we stopped to let the children out,
where the boulders caught the sound, where we spilled
the coke we'd been tooting from Fresno and swore
that was it, we'd marry, knowing we were that far
from home. And where we relieved ourselves, our hollow promises,
and agreed to raise the children into the bourgeois names
of washed-up empire—Nicholas and Alexandra.
You shucked your promises with stalks of wheat
I said I'd carry as a bouquet, and all of us heard
that choir singing in the rocks, angels we thought, sobbing,
or the tabernacle choir rehearsal gone astray and echoing
this far from home. The children were afraid
until you broke all your promises, which was your way,
and memory lasts longer than truth. I left
the fragile and golden wheat
on the dashboard of my old Alliance
when it was hauled to the junkyard in Spook Hollow,
shame of a name, outside the town where the wind

makes the small sound, a hollow sound, as of the sound
made by breath across empty gourds
or land
or the sound pulsing beneath a storm, beneath electrical wires,
beneath slabs of concrete lining front yards,
a sound just between stone and earth, like the low whistle
in the scar pockets the body
forms around foreign implants, the roar of insistent blood
the moment before we faint, which may be
what we hear before we die,
may be what you heard before you died,
still man, quiet man,
after you no longer heard
the voices that kept trying to call you back to the road.

MY DAUGHTER REJECTS WALT WHITMAN IN HER MOTHER'S LIBRARY

> *If for thy father asked, say thou hadst none;*
> *And for thy mother, she alas is poor.*
> Anne Bradstreet

> *her wounds   came   from the same source as her power*
> Adrienne Rich

No chiseled or blocked black letters
        on quality red- or gilt-edged
onion skin, sewn in leather-bound
        volumes on built-in library shelves
for this self-taught Canadian girl.
        I cut teeth in milk-ice figures
on the spare lot rink my father cultivated
each winter. From late October on

he spent his evenings spraying a fine
        layer of water from the garden hose,
patiently preparing a solid page
        of ice inscribed with the dried history
of summer's frozen grass and stubble.
        From figures looped in spins and arabesques
to hockey speed on bobskates,
we bobbed and weaved until gypsies

called spring down the boulevard
        and my mother danced
the chicken in the living room
        to "Ain't Nothin' But a Hound Dog."

Mom finger-rolled my ringlets and smocked my frocks.
    In real life, the princess became a queen,
my sister had the Coronation dolls to show for it,
but I began to get the drift chewing over

commercial messages in French and English
        on my cereal boxes. *A clever girl,*
that Anne Bradstreet, *a literate father*
        with a taste for history, and a library
where a toddler girl in gray flannel
        and cotton pinafore could climb up library stairs
to take down a volume if she were quiet enough.
My father's knee was not for such lessons.

Alone I'd finished the family's
        Reader's Digest condensed novels
at home before I found *The Little House*
        on the Prairie in the town library.
Later the poets I came to love confessed
        they owed their knowledge of the past
to their fathers. What they then had to cast
off, wintry layers as bulky as down, boots, mufflers,

those sweet eager girls reared
        on the classics under dad's thumb
or belt before they fell into their own deep thoughts.
        I had hard knocks,
scarred lips and scabbed knees when I broke form
        against the uncertain homemade
ice, timed my rhythms to the rectangle of white
banked in snow boundaries, backward and forward,

learned how far one's own power could drive her
        when dad demonstrated spread eagles only
limited by his own physics,
        round and round the rink.
This snowy afternoon my daughter thumbs
        through Shakespeare looking for
a soliloquy by a woman who isn't wimpy.
She scans *Taming of the Shrew* and decides to read

Kate's final speech for her school competition,
        hoping her voice will register
an adequate degree of sarcasm. She picks
        among other volumes, chronologically arranged.
"Oh, that Walt Whitman. He gives me the creeps."
        Finished with the printed word,
she cranks up rock and roll in the kitchen
and we dance together to "I Want to Come Over."

Some hit song on the radio, and I'm
        driving cross-country again, this time
time on my side, wide open road, long
        loss of land behind, and whose song
am I singing? Why not test bombs here
        in Nevada, never had a chance, this cheer-
less landscape flanking the endless strand
        of black highway, a little crazed with old tar and
frost crackling against the edges. Lovelock.
        I stop for coffee at a sleazy casino. Talk
stops a second, just a second. I find a corner.
        Nevada. Lovelock, Nevada. I am your mourner.

Here they all are, the people of Nevada. Locked
        in love? First, the waitresses, as they clock
in, complaining impatiently about the graveyard
        shift, flicking menus resolutely spotted with gravy,
halfheartedly taking orders from strangers, not
        apparently giving even the least thought
to the way the hills in this one-horse town
        look as though the wind had filed them down,
like the teeth of horses made to look young,
        and so unlike me undeceived by the tongue
of road licking its way westward, frosted
        breath riding like hope above the smoke of exhaust.

And the linecrew comes in jingling coins into one-
        armed bandits, winning maybe, and having a little fun
flirting with the waitresses skirting their tables who
        are married to men just like them, they know, but who

are not their wives. But hell, this is life here
        in Lovelock, Nevada. Well, something near
enough the soaps, maybe. Hope is something
        that moves through town in a car like mine, singing
some song this America doesn't know. Old snow
        doesn't deter the old couple from showing
up either, neither having risen before noon,
        ordering cottage cheese in unison, the tune

of habit, the tenor of the familiar, but still
        married, damn it, and damn well will be until
death; and then I see the well-dressed woman leave
        with her dwarf twins, and I can't believe
she can believe in anything but keeping the set
        of their faces just so as they all get
into her car and go clear into the hills, frowning
        away fear of the past. *Murder by drowning.*
Ladybug, ladybug, fly away home. Your house is
        on fire, your children all "Gone," he says
to the waitress as she brings their cottage cheese,
        "Gone to England." Sing. No misgivings. I'm getting out.

Full dark now, unroomed and unmoored,
        zooming down the highway toward
any future anywhere here in America, headlight
        sheering across the black ice like mica, brights
pushing into the lonely road like desire, the whole
        criss-cross countryside the same old
Exercise in familiarity, tricks of similarity:
        Sky, mountains, road, the unnerving clarity
swerving to miss some dark animal caught
        briefly in this abandoned stretch, but not
unhappy here where America needs poetry, exhausting
        the road west just before the turn-off to Austin.

1996
I haven't the capacity for war
within. To be sure I have spent nights
leading tours of ancient ravaged territories
spread out beneath my heart, *omphalos*, thighs,

and *mons veneris*, deep probes into the town
where talk is cheap though volumes richly rise
to an occasion. No alarum sounds.
No silken tents pull up against their guys.

(Which is not to claim they lie in wait,
nor wait to lie nor even that they lie,
though lay they may in love's labored estate.)
Then lost? Oh, no. Indeed, I declare a tie!

The point? It is, my love, for you to make
a soldier's pact to keep our peace at stake.

1990
A soldier's pact to keep our peace at stake,
and wouldn't you know, a Gulf War, Desert Storm.
Anyone who'd read *Brave New World* knew how to take
this rhetoric: War is peace, and peace means war.
Flashback to more than twenty years before:
In Stockwell Hall we hung up butcher paper
along the basement walls, ironic fore-
ground to the War Memorial raised much later

bearing names that then were only birthdates
attached to numbers making order out of war
by chance. We swallowed rhetoric and penned
the fates of brothers, boyfriends, last night's dates
in their proper places. We prayed for peace.
We knew back then that war is not an end.

1968
We knew back then that war was not an end.
The end for us too often came in blood
tests, broken hearts, missed periods, a flood
of recriminations, "I'll always be your friend."

Ah, friend. Comrade in arms. What foreign mud-
hole could keep us safe? Yellow-belly earth,
hot mama, warless, giving birth
to future slick-booted camouflage, dry scud

missiles. Slow-tongued and breath-baited,
having no capacity for war, we were fit.
And slogan laden, belly up we waited.
In making love not war we did our bit.

September fourteenth was lottery number one.
Of those who served, I can remember none.

1969
Of those who swerved I can remember none
who chose to swerve only to swerve for fun.
My god, looking at those photos one
would think our days were nothing more than sun-

filled rah-rah ha-ha autumn
all the doo dah day plaid glad spun
candyflake five cylinder motorcycle vroom
vroom and we're outa here, joystick, gan-
ja stick, nickel bags, zigzags, one-
cent sales for speed and mescaline, *The Sun
Also Rises*, *The Two Hands of God*, *One
Flew Over the Cuckoo's Nest,* grade inflation,
hell no, we won't go, Johnson,
a fuck, a wedding, a dubious graduation.

1972
A fuck, a wedding, a dubious graduation.
The "war" brought to a dubious end, disgrace
in our time, and I a wife (B.A.), our nation
embittered, littered with the paper faces

of refugees, dead students, antiwar posters.
It's wedding gifts that make a house a home.
Matching towels, double bed sheets, coasters.
(Five years earlier, I'd made a trip to Rome.

My teacher/guide arranged a date for me
with a Roman racecar driver twice my age.
He bribed the bouncer at the famous Pipeline
to let me in to disco on the stage.

"Bambina! Oh, baby!" The floor lights made my dress
transparent:) Power. Doubt. Desire. Secrets.

transparent): Power. Doubt. Desire. Secrets.
Before we met, my love, I'd say, "Blue moon,"
and never have an inkling I had set
a time, nor committed to a phenomenon
of mutual significance, no less.
No, more. Twice times full, double lun-
acy, ace in the hole, secret asset,
blue moon, blue eyes, blue bottles, blue—why, you.

Secrets): Desire. Doubt. Power. transparent
once in a long long while   a sigh of relief
night sigh   watery cry of a river loon
(name me): a bird, a rock, a star, a leaf,
pluck your terms from the airs apparent,
My Love, My Loon: my once in a blue moon

1965

My love, my loon: once upon a blue moon
we knew so little of love's sky-forged armor,
believed true men can but try, a swoon
small bounty paid in recompense for ardor.

Small bounty paid in recompense for ardor,
our burning question then was would you French kiss?
Primed for adoration, not on fire to adore,
we wouldn't commit our tongues to foreign twists.

We wouldn't commit our tongues to foreign twists,
blithely unaware that we'd been born

into a tongue already twisted to be fit
by screws to one to whom our love was sworn.

We are born to guilt when we are born to tongue.
Innocence? Do not confuse it with the young.

1972
Innocence? Don't confuse it with being young.
Love, I was young when I began to lie.
It came so easily, I swear that I
was as surprised as the friends I was among,

a husband, a couple sets of newly marrieds,
out to hear Teegarden and Van Winkle
and see a psychedelic slide show. Carried
away I cried, "Oh, no. Not that! I think I'll—"

The lie was out before I planned it: that nude,
there on the screen, I claimed, was yours truly.
Tee and Van had taken it, I said, before I knew
the man I'd married. How could they do this to me?

A quick glimpse of the odalisque had flicked past.
Everyone believed they'd seen my ass.

1973
Bet your ass, everyone believed I was
an Ikette before becoming a grad school wife.
At academic parties, I'd swing my ass
in the Tina Turner strut, dig my high

heels into the rug, shimmy, popcorn, four-square,
do all the gestures to "Proud Mary," and ooh-ooh.
(This lie, however, had a double layer,
so I fooled myself with the impromptu

ambush of my endangered territories.)
Less agile wives and thwarted female students
lined up to learn. Oh, I could tell them stories,
respected now as a counter-insurgent.

From then on I was always expected to dance
to make it on my own recognizance.

1988
To make it on my own recognizance
traveling across country, incognito
so to speak, and knowing in the glance
of sun off the dimmed neon Nevada casino

sign (Open 24 hours, Cocktails)
I hadn't a prayer, a pocketful of live
ammo to accompany me into the fray, stale
smoke, cowboys.   I'd swagger in that dive,

chin cocked, convinced, insouciant, perhaps
convincing, that I was not a road-burned woman,
an ordinary Joe, but look—jeans, boots, cool hat:
Aspiring Rock Star. Devil may care. No man

questions the composure of a musician.
You might have seen me watching VH1.

1996
You might have seen me watching VH1
while cooking dinner, with my daughter doing
homework in the kitchen. When Eric Clapton's
backup singer begins her soulful ooh-ing

I tilt my cleaver to the screen and say,
"That's who I really am." The truth out now.
Her voice comes up from territories that lay
too long uncultivated, too long fallow,

barely restrained, modulated, washed of pain
that once was there but turned to love. My thin
voice is dry philosophy. Am
I not that woman underneath my skin?

My daughter looks from singer back to me.
For a moment, then, she studies something closely.

1958
For a moment, then, I study something closely.
I draw the book under the light. It's *War
and Peace*. I am utterly unaware
of the night closing in, of the ghostly
man's figure taking shape in the clothes
that hang from the dry cleaner's mangle
across the street. Empty-armed, they dangle.
A child, I put aside my book morosely.

Truth to tell, I was a little tongue-tied
by what was taking shape beneath my eyes,
my slogans billowing outward from the core.

If love is war, the enemy's allied
to lovers' volumes'-worth of novel lies.
I haven't the capacity for war.

MY DAUGHTER READS ME A POLITICAL POEM OF THE NINETIES

When she asks me, I say I think I will come back
        a sea lion in the Oregon Game Preserve. Young men
will toss me fish. Magnificently fat and tawny,
        I'll be comfy as a worn brown velvet couch.
I'm eating lentil soup and reading *Cooking Light*
        while middle age grows old. One crisp fall morning,
as if she were my own fears, a tawdry squirrel
crazed with thirst careens between my Tempo's wheels,

a deliberate suicide, as I drive down Hawthorne Street.
        Friends fail, their knees, hearts, and parents giving out.
Their children have been given licenses to drive
        themselves into oblivion. My feet grow to look
like Oriental succulents, like gingerroot,
        my nose a big bottomed pear, not ruby Bosc, but Bartlett.
I consider the recipe for pears in ginger sauce, and lick
my finger to turn the page just as my mother might.

My daughter props her book up on the table. *Listen*
        to this one, Mom. She reads a poem that ends "Fuck
the world." Last fall, we drove up Allmost Country Road
        late afternoons so she could ride her paint, Eternal
Cowboy. A cobalt sky took in a dusty sun.
        Having poured its heart out the summer long, it was
outdone by nature's corresponding inner gold
technically dead: the leaves, the horse's mane, my daughter's

hair like copper accolades across her face. I planted
        my heels in the quaking earth as half a dozen horses

thundered down the mountain after her. Flash
        of red and gold, she reined in and flicked her crop
at Perpetual Lucy, Forever Gundy, and Diablo.
        If my daughter were an animal, she would be a horse,
bucking, farting, galloping over the Appalachians
at her first chance. I strain to articulate,

my parched tongue tethered to the rhetoric of beauty,
        when my heart rears up in my throat. Wind in trees sets up
such a noise. A burst of birds reels from hemlocks for all
        the world like applause—or is it laughter? She doesn't know
me in my blue jeans leaving home at seventeen.
        Peace, I raised my fingers in the famous sign
and marched along South University and State.
My concerns were universal: Where have all

the flowers gone and Do I dare to eat a peach?
        The ROTC building burned. Black Panthers, White Panthers,
and Rainbow People glided through the jungle of my youth.
        Who knew then that living meant accommodating
everlasting beauty? Closing her book, my daughter
        leaves. It's all the same to me, applause and laughter,
the waterfall appraisal of my waning thought,
wind shivering leaves gold despite this year's drought.

REVISION

God knows the road's open
to anyone with wheels and a fistful
of cash to cover the hike
in gas since the last oil spill. Some

gone west can't stay put, coming
back, digging in,
settling for the bright scarf
of river, brocaded hills tufted with buttonwood

and rhododendron, the patina of grime
mantling the oldest buildings in the New World.
Some gone west cower below the Wasatch, go
thirsty for trees, dry up

outside the penny's-worth of shade.
Too, too much sky, they gasp through cracked
lips rubbed shiny with fruit gloss from the drugstore.
Bony fingers point to red buttes and angel-less pinnacles

balancing rocks like obsolete language. Once gone west,
I read the grapes shriveled to raisins in my palm,
my life irredeemable.
                         Some born midway
negotiate the old interstates under massive

reconstruction, singing with the window
rolled down through Kansas, Colorado, and Nevada. They turn
their bandannas from babushkas to do-rags
or their hair grows classy, striped the precise reds

of Bandalier and Moab. Some, before they get to L.A.,
shimmy in their blood's private rhythms, stalled
in twelve lanes that spill
the hopeful, the tired, the seedy, the small

successes toward the Pacific stoically licking
the west into the exotic. My daughter gone west
will tune her guitar at a desert comfort
stop and offer her love songs to the looping road.

for Alexandra

HER SONG, CHEMOTHERAPY

Wearing my lace dress, gold shoes and my wig,
I passed through the halls of the anonymous Hilton,
passed by the rooms of anonymous guests,

their beds being changed by childish housemaids.
One housemaid sang loudly, a foreign young girl
in a foreign hotel room singing a song

of ruddy young mangoes clustered on trees.
She sang the few Spanish words I could catch,
tossing them up in the sheets that she billowed,

billowed above the big double bed, the big double bed
in the Hilton. She sang.
Her hair caught in two braids, her uniform too short,

her voice no more than a tremulous quaver,
she sang with joy from some other country
where streets ended in meadows, meadows ended in seas.

She sang and I thought of my recurrent sickness.
I thought of my hair falling out in great handfuls,
falling out that morning in a room down the hall,

falling out on the pillows, the sheets and the tiles,
my hair trailing like fishnets across my shoulders, like veils.
She sang in a voice so weak and unlovely,

I thought of her sisters hardly younger than she was
who still worried about papa and who shinnied up trees
or gathered ragweed and goldenrod from unsullied meadows.

Gold fleur-de-lys on red woolen background, the carpet
muffled my steps as I slipped down the hall,
wearing my lace dress, gold shoes, and my wig,

I listened to her song in the cold-surfaced Hilton,
I listened to her song ignorant of my illness.
It took me much farther along than that morning

I had thought I was ready to go.

I REMODEL NANCY CARDUCCI'S HOUSE

"A finer house than prose"
Emily Dickinson

This is by no means my best trick, adapting
the first idea of someone else long lost
so what I'm left to work with is "a common
family dwelling," an aging house, nothing
more spectacular than measured rooms
of myopic possibilities: Four walls,
the doors, the windows here and here, the closets.
I'd rather thumb my dog-eared magazines
in search of ancient recipes interred
in unappetizing paragraphs of black
and white. Each abstract find I hang above
my *mise-en-scene*, clipped to a flautist's lyre.
Once I've auditioned each ingredient,
inspecting like a kerchiefed *stadi baba*
the home-grown produce in the farmers' market,
pinching eggplants, weighing cherries one
by one before I drop them in my bag,
it's time to cook. I must make something out
of this, transform my fresh discoveries
into the delectable. I cluck and cackle.
So far the gaping cracks in surface plaster
have been limned in masking tape and plastic.
The ceiling fell when we removed the pale
and stained wallpaper that had held it whole
above our heads, exposing rough-hewn laths.
We have dissolved the moldings' seasoned varnish
and the 1900s trellis pattern
peeling off in strips of pink and gray.

"Why must we tear down what they made before?"
a poet friend sobbed in his cups one night.
To know rough struts behind the personal,
the style, means we are left to redesign
the standing rooms as if there's nothing new
beneath the sun. I imagine starting
out from scratch, a chicken claw on dry,
cracked ground, pretending not to know, like chicks,
that some invisible and unnamed hand
has strewn the field corn from above. Like sky,
the benefactor's Amish skirt whips up
in wind. Her eyes are trained on stumbling rocks
or blue hills rumbling out and out from fields
awash with black-eyed Susans, timothy,
and Queen Anne's lace. But still, I recycle.
I don't build new. Any good cook knows
that recreation and creation can be
the same. So far we haven't touched the kitchen's
faded fruit adroop in orange and brown
or stripped the paper from the central room,
its Florentine medallions strung like rows
of vague vaginas embossed in cream and gold.
This room is overcrowded now. A forties
Wurlitzer piano, loveseat, lace—
Oh, doesn't it sound cozy? We've contemplated
our color scheme: Porcelain or Zurich?
Linen, Grass, or Brass? To reassure
the ghost of Nancy Carducci, we choose Camellia.
As mistress of this house she lined its walls
with sexual organs of flowers to lift the dark
and narrow spaces. Dame's Rocket, Devil's
Tongue, Wild Flax, Gayfeather, and Phlox
improve the garden. Windowboxes full

of portulacas and begonias, and baskets
of fuschias hanging from the porch preempt
our early spring attention to interiors.
Twelve dozen chocolate truffles wait in rows
alongside eighteen pounds of marinating
flank steak and other makings for a wedding
dinner for the son of friends. We're living
amid the chaos of our dismantling
what was built before our time as if
the nonagenarian house has not been torn
in shreds, its beams aching for stress relief,
its rooms for coordinated colors, and the whole
damn structure needing my internal support.

March opens the door a crack,
       blue-collared crocus poke up, joysticks
              to a video collage at the border

of the doorstep, snapped off in the lions'
       teeth before April took root, dug in, turned
              up the aspirating worms.

And serrated tufts of long-bladed
       grass pock the lawn, untendable
              clutches that circle clusters

of daffodils the pale yellow of hard beaten
       egg yolks, or paper whites, or ruffed
              double blooms flouncing their belled

skirts over the stone wall to greet
       newcomers and passersby. By then the closet
              smells fusty, its décor formerly bright plashes

of purple and blue among variegated dignities of black
       now shabbier than hopes resurfacing
              in the future, arrived at after a long

arduous passage. Each pressed suit
       taken out and examined
              in the clear light of the first balmy day

misses a button, humiliates with threads raveling
            on the shoulder, a stain on the skirt, or gives out
                        at the seat, though the selected garment

delighted us at the height of the season,
            sitting snugly, and in the right
                        light, smartly or at least crisply

in the mirror of the cramped dressing room.
            Our discards banked up
                        atop the old jeans and shoes worn

in—stalwartly—for replacement. Nothing will do
            now, not the silk jacket, the tailored
                        vest, the sage dress sagging

on the hanger. Their bedraggled
            appearance recriminates, "These are
                        all your bad choices." It's spring. We close

the door on them, the blatant sun of change
            beaming kindly on its golden oak,
                        new worlds to conquer crying for attention.

So we go dazzled into our rock garden,
            trying on the distance between
                        trillium and the purple phlox.

AZALEAS

At last! The hot blush of azaleas
                    has spread across the city
            like the anatomy of desire
        as the cold body of winter

allows its breath escape.
                    Once I loved a man so much
            that when he left me for another
        woman, their lovemaking woke me up

at night. This is the logic
                    of the body, the assimilation
            of desire: a year of nights spent
        like theirs, until reason

named the loss November.
                    That harbor turned ice, all ships
            moored beneath archangelic
        grays of clouds. Such inversions

our skies knew then. Innumerable trips
                    to the mountain for gulps
            of sun, all, all ending
        in the senseless plunge to earth

and its dirtiness. Today, years
                    and years into that time's future,
            a burst of blossoms arrives at my door.
        Still warm in their knowledge

of the bright summer, they settle
for less in my arms.
I tour the city, looking
for the precise bush my armful of blossoms

derived from. I cannot count
the varieties of colors of azaleas
in front of shuttered houses,
nor gauge the brilliance of the particular

blossoms at home in my largest vase.
Such distance looms
between the source and my perception—
as if beauty is the fulfillment of desire.

Once during a hard drive from south to north,
I wanted to stop at the Atlasta Motel.
But we passed it, and beyond a turn in the road,
we happened on a view as breathtaking as sex.

I've never regretted pushing on, so it's odd
that for so long I held fast
to the body's sad belief in losses:
we look for what we've left beside the road.

I should have learned then to imagine
more exotically, to accept
the tropical proliferation of unbidden gifts,
or to believe in the unimaginable, to expect

a glimpse of the beyond-desire
around the bend, a throw-me-a-curve
pink at the edges, azaleas at my feet,
still damp this morning.

IMPLICATE ORDER II

It casts you
sly fish
(reckless)

from the edge
there's no
edge

above below air water
hydrogen hydrogen oxygen
nothing f/lies

glittering nor luminous
swim bladder   gills   discerning eye
dead fish   unbred rock

[nominal operative] sun (*named* Apollo) differentiates what
[verbal dynamic] bakes against the lap   lap
wetdrywetdrywetdrywetdry

we do not mind
we should not mind
now you see it now you

ledge/fish/rock
there is/ there is no
what do we

edgeless   do we do
imagine   it casts you   sly sly fish   from the edge
(reckless) (beautiful)

What I Bear

No barrier stands between the material world of science and the sensibilities of the hunter and the poet.

Once we get over the shock of discovering that the universe was not made with us in mind, all the meaning the brain can master, and all the emotions it can bear, and all the shared adventure we might wish to enjoy, can be found by deciphering the hereditary orderliness that has borne our species through geological time and stamped it with the residues of deep history.

Edward O. Wilson, *Consilience: The Unity of Knowledge*

HEEDLESS

Perhaps we love the shore
        because the debris here could not be ours
                no matter how hard our lives.

Or because the long shelf of land
        continues on under the water
            so even here at the edge

of the world the edge is uncertain.
        Perhaps we love that the water rises
            to uncertain levels leaving

and returning. We may love
        the shore as we love the madwoman
            who repeats the same phrase

endlessly, as we love the dying
        who go on living, the traveler
            who promises return.

Here, just here, we leave
        no mark. Spume renders footprints,
            castle, cry the same.

It's all the same
        what we say to the traveler,
            the dying, the madwoman:

Come back, I love you, come back.

ANOTHER AUTUMN

Light brittle as a long life glances
        off headstones, flattens them into
                white sheets on which the expenditure
      of breath is tallied. From this
side of the fence they are no more imposing

than the razor-thin shadows of the wrought-
        iron railings cast across my path—
              so little divides the quick from the dead,
      this light that washes the silver backs
of fallen leaves quicksilver across the pavement

going out the moment the cost of living
        becomes too steep. Yet there are some
              who go on paying, who stretch the moment out
      beyond reason, beyond design, beyond any accident
that makes the light look merely grim.

What accounts for the will
        to continue along the frayed rope
              of sidewalk, staggering, from the cemetery
      toward the reckless beauty
of the red maple blazing ahead?

for my father

NUTS

*'Here is a nut,' said he, catching one down from an upper bough.
'To exemplify, a beautiful glossy nut, which, blessed with original
strength, has outlived all the storms of autumn. Not a puncture,
not a weak spot any where. This nut,' he continued, with playful
solemnity, 'while so many of its brethren have fallen and been
trodden under foot, is still in possession of all the happiness that a
hazel-nut can be supposed capable of.'*

Persuasion, Jane Austen

"How will I know you? You've always had cancer."

10-year-old daughter to the poet who
hopes to be cured by an autologous bone
marrow transplant.

How would we know
ourselves without death
to contend with? Mothered
or motherless? Silk or sin?
Last night's frost rimes
the beds of our gardens.
Three weeks, and we'll be on
the upswing, sky lightening
earlier each morning, hawks
drawing tight circles
above stubble and new mud.
Pronounced all but dead
six years ago, I took up
flying, a scrap of silk,
a tent, a flag, guyless, unpinned
from the mechanics of grave hoists.
Leaves come undone as the disheveled
hair of women dancing,

branches draw lines
not yet read in a favorite poem.
Soon we'll be claiming spring,
thinking within ourselves
thinking within ourselves
seeds crack, the shoots unfurl,
the marrow in the bone
the marrow in the bone.

Seasons melt under my tongue.
Time sticks in my teeth
like poppy seeds. I suck
my gums, an old woman at leisure.
There may be blizzards to come.
Inside the hollow of a great oak,
some provident squirrel unseen
has stored the future:
two hard nuts—
against desire or lack?

Come spring the virulent spread
of gypsy moths may shrivel new leaves,
leave withered trees black, a puckered
swath across the tender hills, brown fields
rasping with cornstalks rubbed by cruel dry wind.

Come spring tight buds may swell
like nubs of new breasts on bark,
azaleas may burst into temperance.

Who would desire the rotten nutmeat,
the rancid oil, acrid on the tongue,

impulse to memory of bygone days?
Who would choose the tear in silk
layers of sky, egg-shaped,
imagine, the size of Europe? Ornate
cities named to fix dead men's victories,
our failures, forever may slide off
our plates into deep, meaningless blue,
slip through the tear in the ozone,
our skeleton history may burn.
We hear charred bones clacking
marimba music in the avenues.
We smell the stink.

But let go: sweetness wells up unbidden
from below earth's infant furze.
My daughter slings her backpack
over her shoulder and heads out
into the frosty dark. She grows
strong under my roof, our dishes
rich and abundant, our garden thriving.
We leave the dark nut to molder
in our damp hollows, blink in the formless light,
spread our wings, our hands, our lips.
Who will we be?

The first birds chortle in the eaves. Maudlin earth
smells commingle: wet leaves, shattered bones,
matted dog hair, cat piss. Winter is an old ache
in the ankles and groin. Creeks muddy and swell
with mountain run-off, the roiling torrent from the last
bad snows. Its deliberate, headlong rush honeycombs rock

beds, gullies fields. Each year's spring cycle rocks
earth on its ear. I would like to believe, like earth,
in renewal, in the quickening of the blood, in the last
blizzard salted away, in maidenhair skirling the scraped bone
of granite escarpments, to believe this new mottled swelling
and catch in my chest parallels earth's own joyful ache

of rejuvenation. For surely the return to youth must ache.
Who'd want it? I make this old frame quake to the beat of "Rock
Around the Clock," hip to "You Oughta Know." Sounds swell.
What we gather about earth's turn is different from what earth
tenders about us—different as smashed rock from crushed bone.
Even so, we spend our days deciding if spinning earth at last will last

out its cycles or if our own diseases will corrupt it to its last
spring. Night sky's lightening, trailing my grim night-aches
across the earth curled beneath me, the knowledge in my bones,
trails into birds' songs, earth's smells. I stay and rock
my pain to me, bone-pain that is not pain that is of the earth
that feels no pain, rocking myself in my bed where pain swells

niggling as long-haired Lepidoptera eggs laid in July swelling
each spring into molesting Gypsy Moths, niggling as guilt. Last

spring, we waved the banner "Love Your Mother," green earth
on blue water, protested against toxic waste pollution, ached
to believe every slogan could save us. Today atop Band Rock,
we can almost catch the late tunes of fiddles, harps, and bones,

sweet complicated bluegrass aired above the bleached blue bone
of the Susquehanna, the sweet-water at full spring swell,
the twisted spine of the valley. We tune in some bluesy rock,
dangle our legs over the cliff face in the rosy late last
light. Imagine this no more either by design or by mistake!
I breathe so as not to take my pain as standing for the earth's.

Where does pain end and bone begin? Unconscious earth
itself swells from abstract facts into the face of hard rock.
Unlike the earth, I ache to make each freshening spring my
last.

A repeat of a decade ago, another late spring, a fooler:
By my birthday, trees barely bud up and still
haven't leaved a month later. Hard to tell whether they're dead

with mottled limbs braced against partly cloudy skies.
The crocus up early's been bitten off, while in April the hyacinth
waves rags on sticks. No heady perfume reels us to our kitchen door

this year. Yet daffodils in abundance cling tenaciously, in bloom
a full month, and—saving grace—the purple azalea's arrived.
This ten-year revolution barreled spring to my gardens

at six different houses in town, fueled a revolt in my late-bloomed
spirit. Now I call the valley's circling hills *mountains* and think little
of what's beyond. This year, too, my daughter writes from Boston:

"The day, the sun, the daffodils make me think of you."
For almost the full decade, new late love has kept me
apprised of all the phases of the moon, the revolving

seasons, the state of the earth, changes in weather. This season
he says, "Look, it's the last blue moon of the millenium."
Failures wane, appeased by this finite repetition of fullness.

And why not? Under the usual moon, air fouls into gorgeous sunsets
imitating old loves, and people who manage no better than I
manage care, manage money, manage to believe

that fair weather for pilots will manage the foul. Tonight, under
the blue moon, bare branches silver till we forgive their delinquencies.
We breathe in the ambiguous space opened just in time for us.

Oh, Blue Moon, boon of second chances, of more grace than we deserve!
A ghostly thought filters through, and I look and look as I lean
into him, my blue moon, last of the millenium, of my contentious life.

LENTICCHIE IN UMIDO

The trick here is not to cook the lentils until they fall apart.
They must be tender but still firm enough to hold their
shape.

Lynne Rossetto Kasper, *The Splendid Table*

Off the shelf, the hard-shelled lentils stream
from the glass jar's bulb, their homey clatter
the ticking of humility. I measure fistfuls

of brown, sexless, flat-faced buttons, actual
as summer dirt collected under nails
that have scratched holes in mean clay footing

a fire escape, with bruised lunulae,
eking radishes under interminably blue,
too blue, sky. What a day to cook:

A whiteout, any imaginable color
hulked down beneath winter's futile anatomy;
inside, our gold and purple walls anomalous

skins of ripe fruit. *Spread the lentils*
in a shallow baking dish. Capon broth
cooked gently (*Say one hundred between each bubble.*),

steeped so long its bones disintegrate.
Our house of broth, of burgundy flannel sheets,
the high-backed oak bed. She sits cross-

legged, crumpled at the foot, diffident,
defiant, and comes out, her eyes not like modest
lentils, but like shells lodged in the fact

of the sand, like White Sails grown in well-crocked pots:
They start life green, become white, and then revert
again to green with age. Copper bands

of hair flat gone ash in the meager light
allowed in through snow-blanked windows, crackling
static in dry air as she twirls the ends.

The copper stockpot flares red, flame
licking the lip, goes cold. This feels
like the end of cooking, like pots hanging unused,

the creep of cobwebs gathering. This feels
like the end of the crumpled page I smooth out to the plane
of sand in a flat landscape, hands brown,

aggravated, digging at the roots of duneweeds sprouted
under the moon, tearing them away for love, for love.
What would it have been like for her to grow

up in the empty mouth of a scream
as the child in Nova Scotia still recalls:
Now there is no scream. Once there was one

and it settled slowly down to earth one hot
summer afternoon; or did it float
up, into that dark, too dark, blue sky?

But surely it has gone away, forever.
I mark the middle of my life as where
the white begins to turn back into green,

and I am now the she. I am the mother.
I wore the mauve garter and push-up bra,
I spread my legs. I played the loony, the victim,

the flat-out unloved long enough to believe in it,
then laid away my scream in the waste brimming
the ocean. I conceived my child. Cooked her up.

Plotted. Potted. She unwinds from the end
of the bed, scuffs away. My love for her
is datum, a lentil. She's had it. Now she gives

me leave to unfold the scream from my adolescent
nightgown, to shake from it the darkest blue.
I must be everything I want myself.

Still in no time her image coalesces
in fragrant beads of steam hovering above lentils,
her eyes the beautiful white sails, filling the house

as all her life, like all of mine, has blackened
my pages. Why not? We have had a blizzard.
Were we to venture out we'd write that *ashes*

smudge the shoulder-high banks of snow. As if
our icy walks don't scare enough, the plow
has crossed the paths we shoveled for ourselves.

And now there will be no getting through.

———

ll. 13-15: *The Splendid Table,* Lynne Rossetto Kasper

ll. 23-24: Simon & Schuster's *Complete Guide to Plants and Flowers*

ll. 39-43: "In the Village," *Collected Prose*, Elizabeth Bishop

ACTUARIAL TABLES

Primary Causes of Death

1. *Overloaded Memory*
   She dies in her sleep, tomorrow a door
   closed against a closet crammed with sports
   equipment, coats for every season, roller blades, a pink boa,
   gardening gloves, binoculars. The invitation
   to the Arts Council ball flutters to the floor beside her bed. No Cinderella,
   she will not rise from her father's ashes.
   The water glass is half empty, one corner of the crossword incomplete
   Her child has tuned her paisley guitar to play
   a new song about new love, and her lover
   has forced paperwhites in a jar of colored stones.
   Her memory overflows into a cave where her footsteps end.
   Her last thoughts: Where did I leave my car keys,
   dog's grooming appointment on Monday, bank closed
   Wednesday afternoons. Library closes early on Fridays.
   Bills due the first, tenth, fourteenth, twenty-second, and thirtieth.
   Spring water delivered every other Thursday. Trash picked up on Fridays.
   Her daughter's lengthy monologue about a tangle with a checkout clerk
   shuffles in her ear's coil beside her lover's reports
   from the workplace and her uptown friend's third repeat
   of a story about her former hairdresser's home remedy for cramps.
   No room. No way out. That's life.

2. *Lack of Imaginative Experience of Afterlife*
   You failed to know there are no
   borders between this life, so-called,
   and the next, so-called.
   You failed to imagine

The next ten or possibly twenty-six dimensions
of self.
You did not learn metaphor, the language of the afterlife.
the language of heaven, god, rest in peace, physics.
You had no art.

3. *Keats Syndrome: Negative Capability*
Epicurus tells us: "Ethics deals with things to be sought
and things to be avoided, with ways
of life and with the *telos*."
Keats settled into avoidance, denial, happy
not to struggle
with the "irritable" need to know.
Live and learn.

4. *Abuse*
Close your eyes, child. Long
grass brushes your cheeks pressed to earth.
A palpable sun. Sidewalks crumble away
in gray cities. Lie down.
This is your home.

5. *Suicide*
The door opens to a wall.
The road dips down.
The grade is steep.
You are sliding in rocks and twigs.
Arms is a dead metaphor.

6. *Trash*
In the landfill.
On the television.

In eighteen-wheelers decked in numbered diamonds, circling
    the No HAZMATS zones.
On talk shows.
In self-help vanity publications with seven typographical errors per page.
On unused athletic fields in winter.
In the gutters.
On my front yard: *Frontier* cigarette packs, Busch beer cans, $1,000,000
    candy bar wrappers, pretzel bags, diapers, condoms.
In the refrigerator, disguised in plastic.

7. *Abuse of Power*
    An ache, a welling up of tears,
    each time lies come uncovered, or due praise sleeps, denied or misdirected,
    or a gender, a race, a scholar crumples like trash blown across
    an urban parking lot in a cunning wind.
    The toll on nervous systems, pain receptors.
    The pond ices over. A purple scarf freezes to the underside of the layer
    of ice.
    In spring, it floats free.
    Crippled, frazzled,
    it distracts us from the objects tangled in the weeds below. Our losses.

8. *Poetry*
    Imagined death. Case in point:
    The poet wrote: "He had been drinking steadily
    all week,/ And was dealing cards/ When the muscle of his own heart/
    Kicked him back so hard in his chair its wood snapped."
    That is how it happened to him. Precisely. Found with his word
    processor turned on, he must have been playing
    solitaire, the game of his life, and drinking bourbon
    from an eight-sided glass of prunted crystal.
    Statistics show
    he recalled his own lines as he fell back

if he had time. He had no time
to think, *"I have won the argument
with death."*

[*Addendum: No Coverage*]
   Terrorism
   Here I am. Come get me. I'm in the tower I've built,
crouching behind dumpsters of apathy, barrels of greed,
the carelessness of my vote. Kids! (You gone blind
in our textile mills. Shepherds leading your flocks across the mines):
Listen to the whistle of the misguided missiles
Bypassing your hearths. What are you waiting for?
Haven't we sold you enough guns to destroy all of us yet?

Factor risk in space allotted below:

> *The reason why the hairs stand on end, the eyes water,*
> *the throat is constricted, the skin crawls and a shiver runs*
> *down the spine when one writes or reads a true poem is*
> *that a true poem is necessarily an invocation of the*
> *White Goddess or Muse, the Mother of All Living, the*
> *ancient power of fright and lust—the female spider or*
> *queen-bee whose embrace is death.*
>
> Robert Graves, *The White Goddess*

Honey, your idea is rooted, *tant pis,*
in the male root, this time not *mal* but you know,
stem or stick, dick, *pièce de persistence*, penis.
Thar [s]he is blowing!

Rising from its falling to its previous heights,
powered up red, hard, from a wan and pink flower,
lying limply, harmlessly. I admit it:
Nothing's quite like it.

And it cheers me up just to see the tender
flaccid lily taken in hand, so to speak.
Thus it is I sympathize, can imagine,
get a weak grip on

its innate philosophy, where it came from,
even though I find myself closed to its charms,
on the wrong side, passively speaking, of it.
I am excluded.

It's the fact of it, my dear, that explains why
men have better memories than their women,
thus, as Plato explained it, they have better
heads on their shoulders.

Once you lose your memory, kiddo, you lose
your godgiven faculty of thought, perchance
lost to dream. Hmm. There it is: *le petit mort*.
Dead and then risen,

granted there's some chick around willing to jog
old memories, *frotter le peur*, jump the old bones
(Are you feeling hairs on your neck rise, sweetie?),
do a mnemonic

jig. The upshot: Memory is desire and
therefore desire memory. Beauty commands
death to exist. However, not so my scars
failing to swell from

little puckered tucks to malevolent breasts
giving some male something to muse about. Nope,
private parts of feminine bodies make change
permanent in time:

breasts lopped off for once and for all, lips sewn shut,
clitorises severed by tribal doctors
so that virgin women of marriageable
age cannot find out

what it is to fuck or that to fuck is to
know. But independent of genitalia,

women, oddly, still seem to think they're women,
nourishing children,

packing off grown kiddies to college, though
somewhat, oh, less easily, shall we put it
delicately, amused or as amusing
deprived of their clits.

No, my body indicates time moves forward,
not in cycles worth the attention of rite,
or in wreckage relevant to the rise of
beauty from losing.

Boredom, *en tout*, rankles in veilless brides who
cease to take delight in their bridegrooms' simple
glee in finding that the same thing will happen
over and over,

thereby giving credence to faith that glory
rises from the past, that the sun will come up,
memory takes precedence over beauty
created from change.

Putting on her earmuffs, the wife hauls empty
bottles to the recycling center, clockwise
working, knowing sticky remains all too well.
Patterns she sees lie

horizontal, crossing her sex and mother
earth, under tyranny of memes, telltale
imprint of progenitorship. The smog dims that
sun, and the trash builds

up in harbors. Reservoirs are polluted.
Her breasts sag, her resources used up, walls grown
dry and thinskinned, papery, fragile. No blood,
nothing to draw sharks.

She'll lose to the tick of the dick, to youth of which there's
always more, she knows, offering planets to old
sticks in mudholes. If not, so what, the old sticks
reason it. Who would

want to linger here on this planet if it
can't be as it was for our fathers? Today,
thirteenth anniversary of my first mas-
tectomy, makes my

will to change, my change of life, seem like small change.
No one's muse, I am amused by the full cup,
change purse, sow's ear, *soutien-gorge* (breast prop), *tous sans
mementos moris*.

I have disappointed my men beyond all
measure looking willfully for the poem
outside pain, truth undaunted by swordplay, beauty
free of the past. My

new world gleams before me as hard and smooth
as a tooth, a gum, or a bone I'll become
leaving this old world for a future without
sticky reminders.

BEAUTY/TRUTH

The laurel's past blooming
at World's End. Leaves settle
down to decay over winter.
If we believe the myth of renewal,
we will see another spring,
crowned with new growth,
blood liquid, marrow quick in our bones.

Truth is anything we avoid
when we search for faces
of gods above us, and it's beauty
we say we believe we see
in their faint expressions.

It may be a physics experiment:
A beaker, a dot of indigo ink
in viscous liquid, threads of blue
unwinding, unwinding,
until rewound to the source
and lifted out wholly.

Or it's the spot on the street
we refuse to look toward,
where we know blood stains
the pavement, left
from yesterday's accident.
Or it's sorrow.

Though we hardly contemplate it,
the afterlife absorbs us. Tonight,
an enormous sun taints mountains pink,
a puddle of clouds dissipates,
and the light, evaporating, leaves us.

As if one by one they lose a grip
on their roost, days let go
until somehow below
us, only young foragers slip,

mistaken and muddled, bereft
of weight. Days float unanchored
around us, life's dreams as well unmoored,
not exactly fragile, but adrift,

leading to predictable ends. Quaint, even,
the daily grind. The wise idea's
an albatross seven years at sea,
moulting and scattering feathers, preening

exotic plumage, blue as our ragged seacoast,
yellow as a toy truck and plum so certain
we say we'll stay on and on.
But by the time that last scrawny claw has loosed

its hold, we're ready to hurtle,
simple hearted and alone
toward gray, leaving love
behind in its oily—beautiful!—swirl.

Ready for flight we neither sleep
nor wake but hold to our perches
until we are so tired of the mess,
so tired we can believe

that truth and peace lie in wait
just outside our cage.

my heart has changed after all
      this time, let me tell you.

Here where no one has set foot
      I want nothing more.

The desert is behind, me, its flowers,
      still, palely trumpeting midnight.

Now that I have no mountains before me,
      the hills have become all my dream,

strength in place of power,
      their blue blurs in sky.

They stand for the way I need
      no word from strangers,

their familiar sprawl
      marks enough for my longing.

Imagination is adequate,
      my empty landscape ruined

archaic mesas and trembling
      rocks, unbalanced.

If I go to my mailbox on the edge
      of the plain, I want to see

no recognizable letters, rest assured.
      Reconciliation is possible,

remember, I have given my word.
      I write now by heart, cross it.

PENELOPE AUSTIN was born in Michigan in 1951. She attended the University of Michigan, the University of Missouri, the University of Utah, and St. Hilda's College of Oxford University. Her first book, *Waiting for a Hero*, won the Devins Award for Poetry in 1988, and was published that year by the University of Missouri Press. Her poem "Eternal Love" was featured as a Poetry in Motion poem on public transportation in Philadelphia and Pittsburgh. Her poems appeared in *The New Republic*, *The Kenyon Review*, *American Poetry Review*, and the book *Poets Against the War*. After living with breast cancer for almost 20 years, she died at her home in 2003.